W9-AKE-246

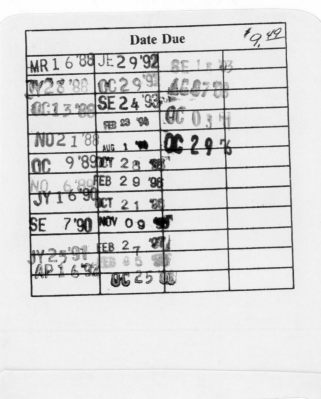

Date Due		$9.49
MR 1 6 '88	JE 2 9 '92	SE 1 s '93
NV 2 8 '88	OC 2 9 '9?	AG 07 93
OC 1 3 '88	SE 2 4 '93	OC 0 3 11
	FEB 23 '94	
NO 2 1 '88	AUG 1 '9	OC 2 9 96
OC 9 '89	OCT 2 8 '95	
NO 6 '89	FEB 2 9 '96	
JY 1 6 '90	OCT 2 1 '96	
SE 7 '90	NOV 0 9 '97	
JY 2 5 '91	FEB 2 7 '97	
AP 1 6 '92	FEB 05 '97	
	OC 2 5 00	

J
646.47   Conaway, Judith
C   Make your own
           costumes and
           disguises

EAU CLAIRE DISTRICT LIBRARY

Make Your Own
COSTUMES
and
DISGUISES

Written by Judith Conaway
Illustrated by Renzo Barto

Troll Associates

EAU CLAIRE DISTRICT LIBRARY

80854

Troll 10/9/87 *9.*

Library of Congress Cataloging in Publication Data

Conaway, Judith (date)
    Make your own costumes and disguises.

    Summary: Provides instructions for making costumes,
disguises, and masks and appropriate props and jewelry
to accompany them, covering characters from cave dweller
to space traveler.
    1. Costume—Juvenile literature.   2. Masks—Juvenile
literature.   3. Make-up, Theatrical—Juvenile literature.
[1. Costume.   2. Masks.   3. Handicraft]   I. Barto, Renzo,
ill.   II. Title.
TT649.C66   1987   646'.47   86-11212
ISBN 0-8167-0840-1 (lib. bdg.)
ISBN 0-8167-0841-X (pbk.)

Copyright © 1987 by Troll Associates, Mahwah, New Jersey
All rights reserved. No part of this book may be used or
reproduced in any manner whatsoever without written
permission from the publisher.
Printed in the United States of America

10   9   8   7   6   5   4   3   2   1

CONTENTS

A DRAMATIC BEGINNING

What if you were one of the first people on Earth? Can you imagine what your life would be like? You would probably live with a small group of people. You would always be on the move, searching for food in the forests.

Do you want to make up a play about the first people? On the next few pages, you'll find ideas for costumes and props. The story is up to you!

CAVE PERSON'S TUNIC

Long, long ago, both men and women wore simple tunics and capes, made from the skins of animals.

Here's what you need:

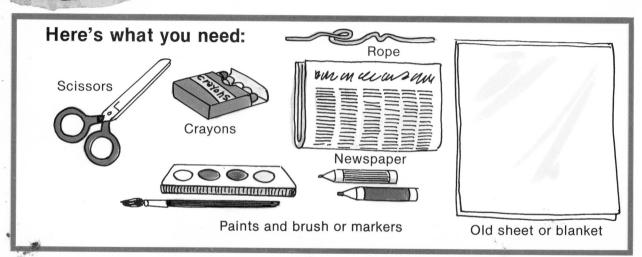

Scissors

Crayons

Rope

Newspaper

Paints and brush or markers

Old sheet or blanket

Here's what you do:

1 Fold the blanket in half and spread it on the floor. Lie down on the blanket, with your shoulders on the fold. Stretch your arms out as shown. Have a friend trace around you to make the tunic shape.

2 Cut out the tunic. Be sure to cut through both layers. (If the material is too thick, cut through one layer at a time. First, cut the top layer. Then, use that layer as a pattern for the one underneath.)

3 Cut a small slash along the folded edge as shown. Then, cut out a small circle for your head to go through.

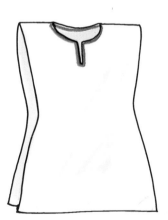

4 Use a rope to tie the tunic around your waist.

Use markers or paints to decorate your tunic to look like animal fur. You may want to cover your work area with newspaper to keep it clean.

Here are some ideas for decorating your tunic:

Mountain-lion fur

Buffalo hide

Deerskin

Wolf fur

STONE-AGE TOOLS

Here's what you need:

Scissors

Glue

Corrugated cardboard

Newspaper

Thin rope

Pencil

Brown construction paper

Broom handle (for spear)

Short dowel (for ax)

Gray and black paints and brush

Here's what you do to make the shaft of your spear or ax:

1 Spread newspaper over the area where you will be working. Lay a piece of brown construction paper on the newspaper. Spread glue over half of the brown paper.

2 Place the broom handle (or dowel) over the glued area. Roll the paper around the broom handle.

3 Wrap thin rope around the paper tube you have just made. Tie the tightest knots you can, so the shaft will stay glued to the handle.

4 Let the glued areas dry completely.

5 Make 2 cuts in the brown paper tube, one on each side of the cylinder.

6 Fold the edges as shown. Set the handle aside and continue to make the ax and spear heads as shown on the following pages.

Here's what you do to make the head of your spear or ax:

1 Copy these patterns, or draw an ax head or spear head of your own. Cut 2 of the head shapes out of cardboard for each tool.

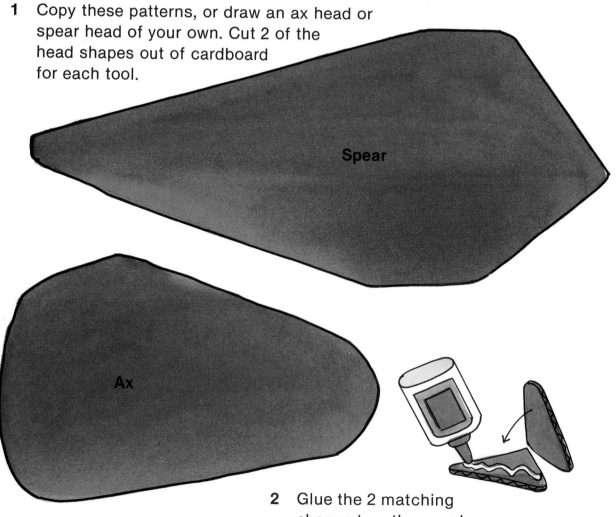

Spear

Ax

2 Glue the 2 matching shapes together as shown.

3 When the glue has dried, paint both sides of the ax or spear head. Paint it gray to look like stone.

Here's what you do to assemble the ax or spear:

1 Spread glue inside the folded ends of the brown paper. Place the ax or spear head between the points of the shaft.

2 Wrap thin rope around both the ax (or spear) head and the shaft, crossing the rope over both as shown. When the glue has dried, your stone-age tool is ready to be used!

For stone-age knives, make a long narrow spear head. Use a paper-towel tube for the handle. Make 2 slits in the tube, and insert the spear head into the slits. Glue it in place. Then, wrap thin rope around the handle and the spear head.

EAU CLAIRE DISTRICT LIBRARY

STONE-AGE BOOTS AND LEGGINGS

Here's what you need:

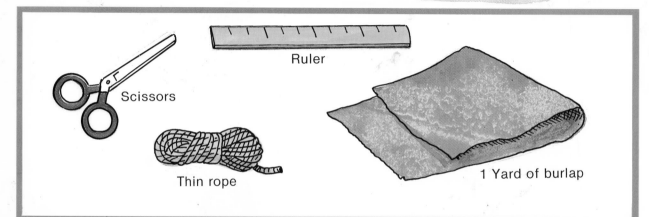

Scissors

Ruler

Thin rope

1 Yard of burlap

Here's what you do:

1   Fold the cloth in half...and then in half again. Cut the cloth along the folds. You now have 4 equal rectangles. Cut 2 pieces of thin rope that are each 24″ long. Cut 2 more pieces that are each 36″ long.

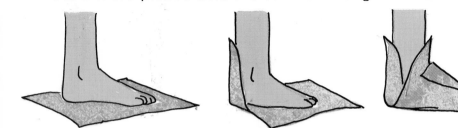

2   Place the heel of your foot at one corner of one rectangle. Fold the back corner up at the heel. Then, fold the side flaps. Last, fold the toe triangle up.

3   Use one 24″ piece of rope to tie each boot just below the ankles. Flap the cloth above the ankle over the rope.

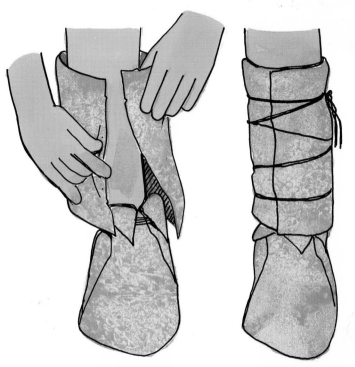

4   Use the remaining rectangles for leggings. Wrap a rectangle around each leg, overlapping the top of each boot. Use the 36″ ropes to lace the leggings as shown.

WILD ANIMAL MASKS

Here's what you need:

Manila file folders

Pencil

Glue

Paints or markers

Scissors

Light cardboard

String

Hole punch

Here's what you do:

 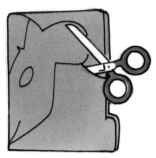 

1 Copy one of the patterns shown on the following pages for your animal mask. Draw the head pattern onto the folder, with the center of the face along the fold as shown.

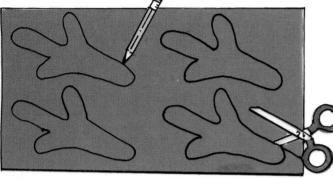

2 Cut out the mask. Cut through both layers of the folder, but do not cut along the fold. Open your mask, and use paints or markers to decorate it. Cut out eye holes. Then, punch a hole on either side of the mask.

3 Copy the pattern for the animal's horns onto cardboard. Cut out 4 horns from the cardboard.

4 Glue each pair of horns together. Do not glue the part of the horns that will be attached to the mask. Slide these 2 ends over the mask with one piece in front and the other in back of the mask. Glue the horns in place.

5 Thread string through the holes on the sides of your mask. Tie the strings to your mask. You're ready to wear your mask!

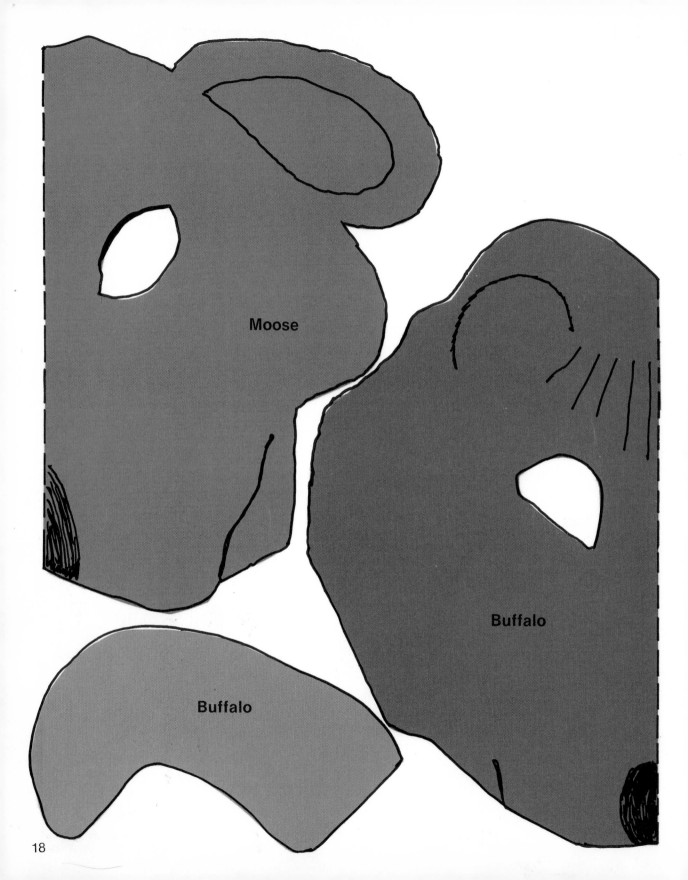

Moose

Buffalo

Buffalo

18

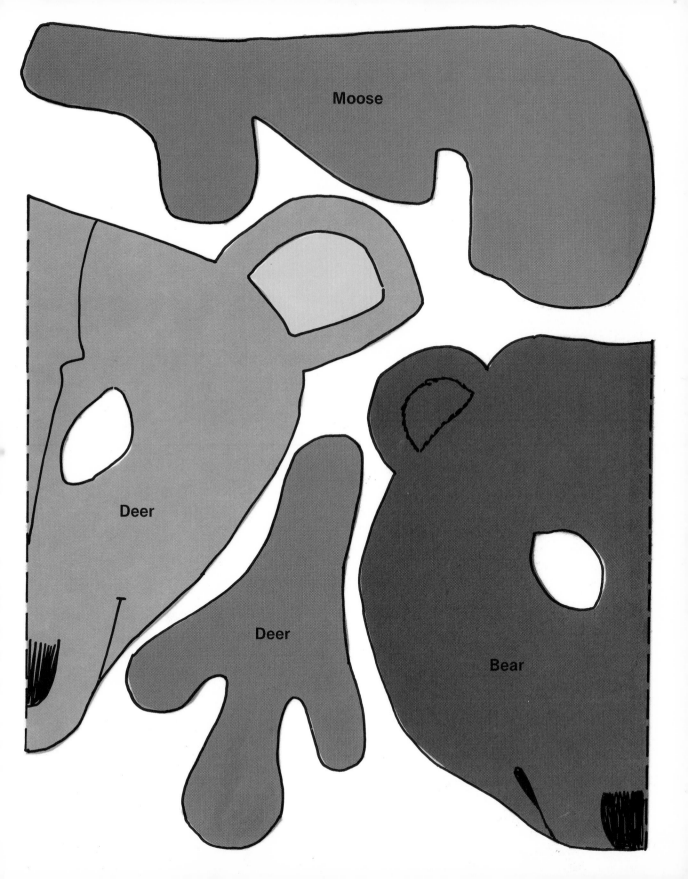

Moose

Deer

Deer

Bear

SETTING THE STAGE FOR CIVILIZATION: GREEK TOGA

More than two thousand years ago, many people had stopped living as hunters and settled in towns and cities. Some of the most important cities were in Greece. Ancient Greece had many great artists, writers, and athletes. You will meet a few on the following pages. All are wearing the same basic costume. It is called a *toga*.

Here's what you need:

Old bed sheet

Markers

Safety pin

Ruler

Here's what you do to make a Greek toga:

1 Fold a sheet in half, lengthwise. Make another fold, about 1 foot down from the first fold.

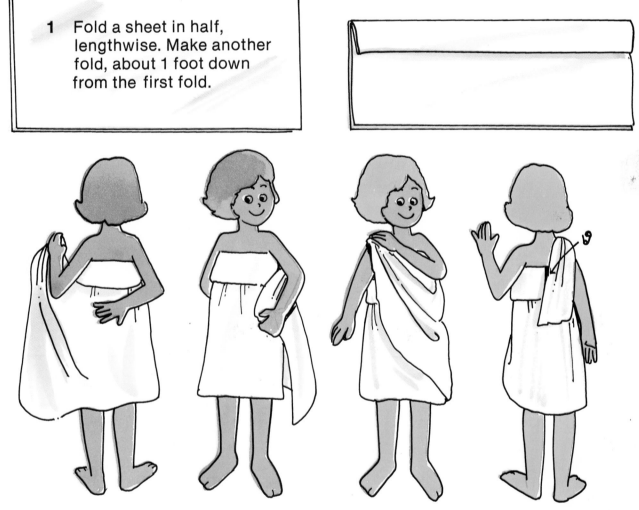

2 Hold one end of the sheet in the middle of your back. Wrap the sheet all the way around you one time. Then wrap the sheet around you again. Flip the remainder over your shoulder.

3 If needed, use a safety pin to fasten the draped end to the sheet layers underneath.

4 If you like, you can draw these border designs on your toga. Use markers to make the designs. **Now your toga is ready to wear!**

GREEK POET'S LYRE

In ancient Greece, singers and poets often played a harp-like instrument, called a lyre, as they sang or read poetry.

Here's what you need:

Scissors

Stapler

Pencil or crayon

Rubber bands

Paper

Ruler

Corrugated cardboard

Here's what you do:

1 Copy the lyre pattern, as shown on the next two pages, onto a folded sheet of paper. Cut through both sides of the paper, but do not cut along the fold.

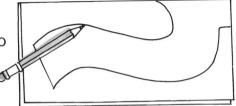

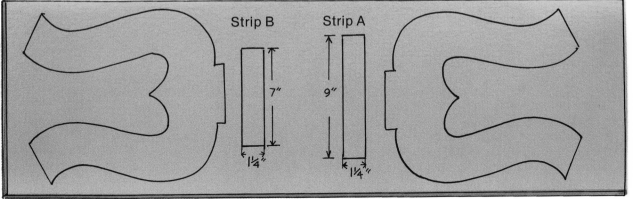

Strip B

7"

1¼"

Strip A

9"

1¼"

2 Use the pattern to trace 2 lyre shapes onto cardboard. Cut out the 2 shapes. Then, cut out 2 more strips of cardboard as shown above.

3 Place the rubber bands around Strip B. Then, lay Strip B across the lower part of the lyre. Adjust the rubber bands, so they lie in front of the open space. Staple Strip B to the lyre as shown. Then, slip cardboard Strip A through the rubber bands. Staple Strip A as shown.

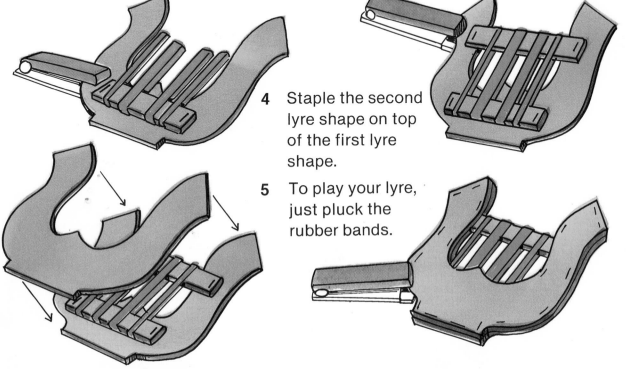

4 Staple the second lyre shape on top of the first lyre shape.

5 To play your lyre, just pluck the rubber bands.

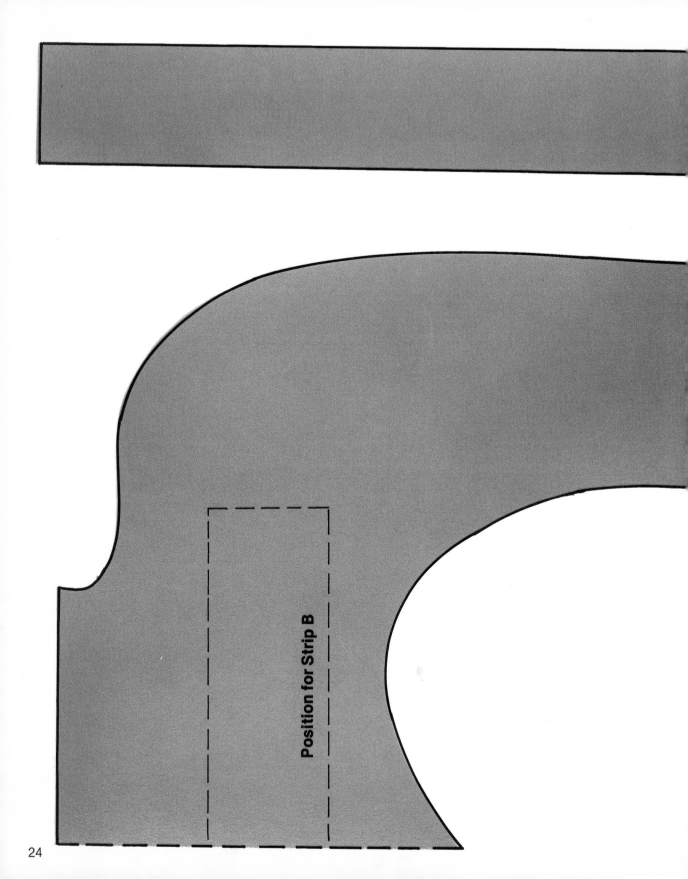

Position for Strip B

24

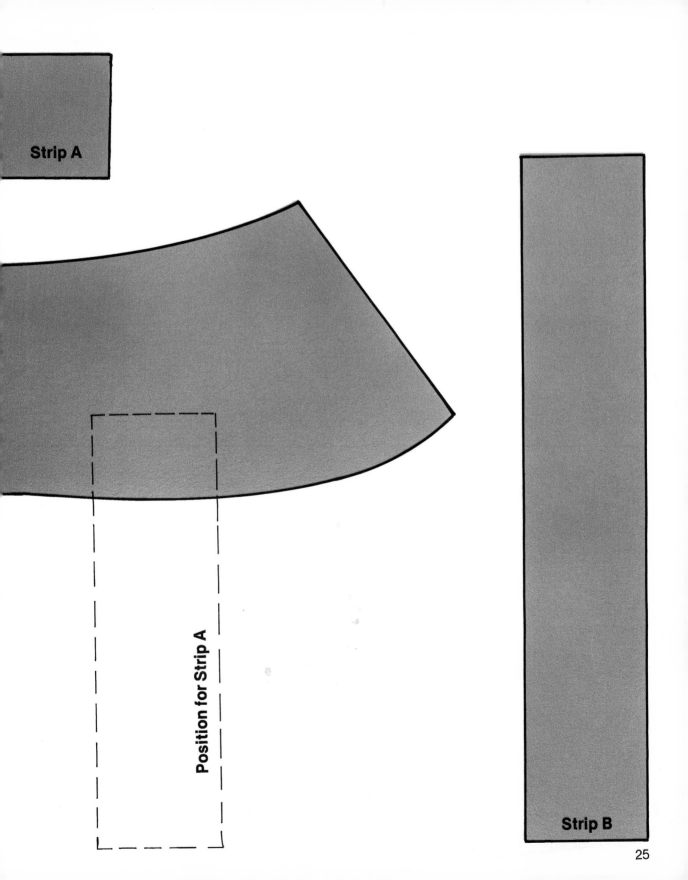

Strip A

Position for Strip A

Strip B

LAUREL WREATH

When a Greek athlete won a contest, he or she was given a laurel wreath as a sign of honor. Why not make a laurel wreath and award yourself a prize?

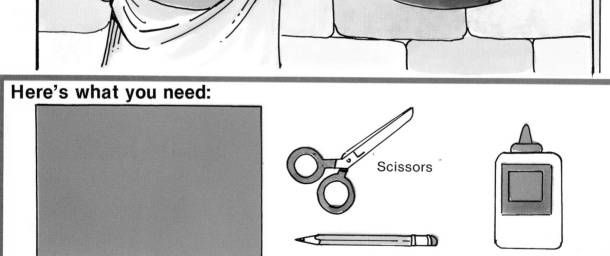

Here's what you need:

Green construction paper

Scissors

Pencil

Glue

Here's what you do:

1 Fold the green paper in half, and cut along the fold.

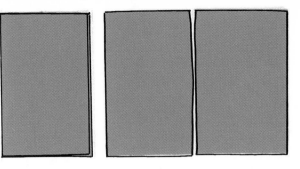

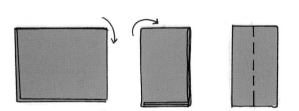

2 Fold each half in half...and in half again. Unfold the paper and cut the rectangles apart. You get 8 rectangles from 1 sheet of paper. Each rectangle forms a leaf in the wreath. Fold each rectangle in half, lengthwise.

3 Copy this pattern. Trace it on the green construction paper. The ce line of the leaf goes along the fold. Carefully, cut out each leaf.

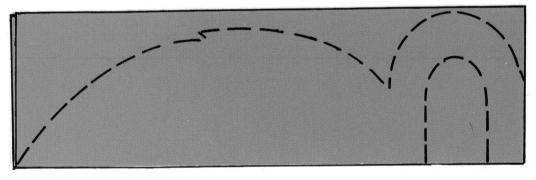

4 To thread the wreath, push a folded leaf through the opening of an opened leaf. Then, unfold the new leaf in the chain.

5 When your leaf chain is long enough to wrap around your head, add one more leaf. Spread glue on the back of the last leaf. Glue it to the first leaf. When the glue has dried, you can wear your new wreath!

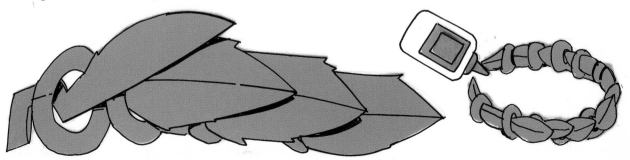

GREEK JEWELRY

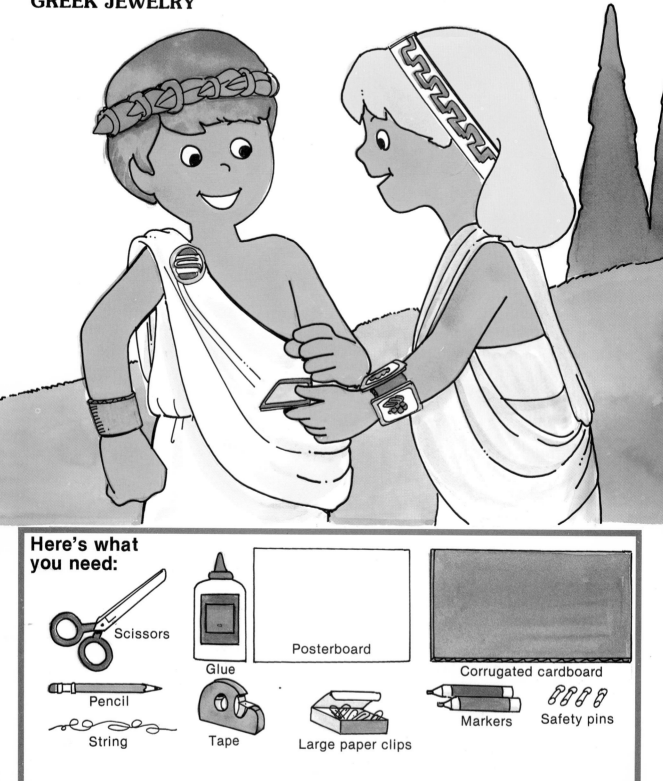

Here's what you need:

Scissors

Pencil

String

Glue

Tape

Posterboard

Large paper clips

Corrugated cardboard

Markers

Safety pins

Double circle

Circle

Lozenge

Here's what you do:

1 Cut small shapes out of posterboard.

2 Use markers to draw designs on the shapes. Copy these designs, or make up a few of your own.

3 To make a Greek pin for fastening a toga, tape a safety pin to the back of one of the shapes.

4 To make a headband, armband, or bracelet, use string to measure the distance around your forehead or arm. Cut a narrow strip of cardboard that is about 1-½ " longer than the string.

5 Glue the decorated shapes to this strip of cardboard. When the glue has dried, wrap the strip around your head or arm. Fasten the band together with tape or paper clips.

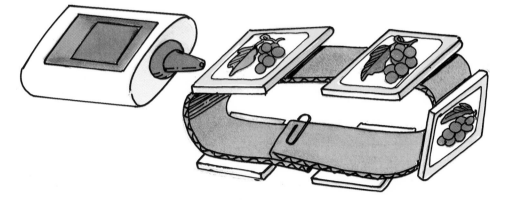

THE MIDDLE AGES: A MEDIEVAL TUNIC

Ordinary people—like Robin Hood—dressed in simple tunics, with knit leggings and furs to keep them warm.

Here's what you need:

Scissors

Rope, cord, or belt

Safety pins

Crayons

Large rectangle of cloth

Here's what you do:

1 Fold the cloth in half as shown. Spread it out on the floor. Lie down on the cloth with your neck along the fold. Stretch your arms out to the sides. Have a friend draw the tunic around you.

2 Cut out the tunic. Be sure to cut through both layers of cloth.

3 Cut a half-circle at the fold line and a small slash in one side of the opening to help you slip the tunic over your head.

4 Use safety pins to pin the seams as shown.

5 To wear the tunic, just slip it over your head. Fasten at the waist with a belt.

Hints:

Tunics should reach just above the knees for men and boys.
Tunics should reach just above the ankles for women and girls.
Be sure to wear sandals, clogs, or moccasins on your feet.
For a winter costume, add leg warmers to the outfit.

DRAGGIN' DRAGON COSTUME

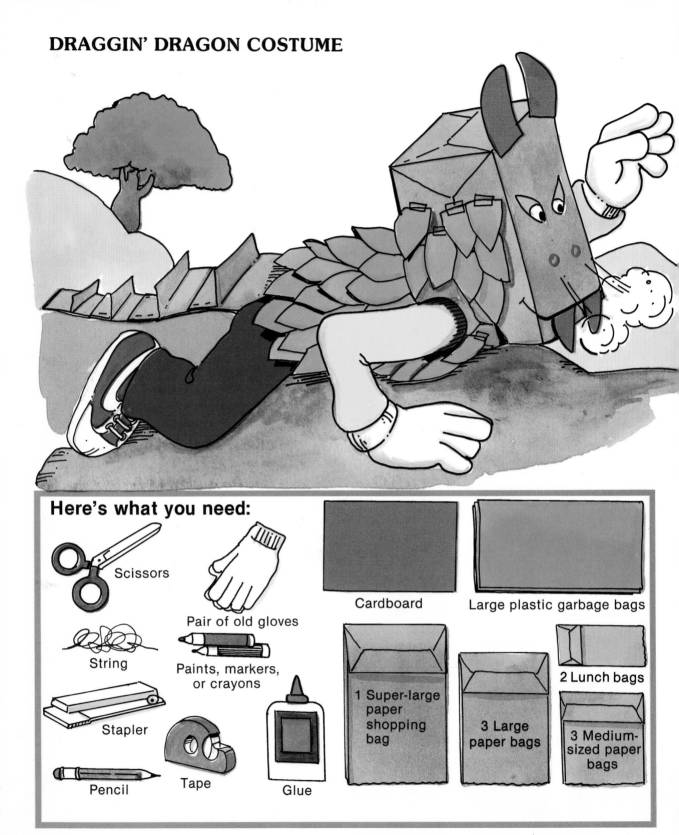

Here's what you need:

Scissors

Pair of old gloves

String

Paints, markers, or crayons

Stapler

Pencil

Tape

Glue

Cardboard

Large plastic garbage bags

1 Super-large paper shopping bag

3 Large paper bags

2 Lunch bags

3 Medium-sized paper bags

Here's what you do to make the face mask:

1 Cut away a piece from each side of the large paper bag as shown.

2 Place the bag over your head. Use a marker to indicate where the eye holes will be. Remove the bag and carefully cut out the eye holes. Cut holes for the nose and mouth in the same way.

3 Use the patterns below to cut out horns and fangs. Glue them in place as shown.

Cut at least 50 dragon scales from the garbage bag.

4 Use the pattern to cut the dragon's scales. Attach the scales to the sides and back of your mask with tape.

Cut 2 horns from stiff cardboard.

Cut 2 fangs from stiff cardboard.

Here's what you do to make the body:

1 Cut arm and neck holes out of the super-large paper bag. Then, cut a straight line up the front of the bag. Try on your "costume" to be sure that it fits!

2 Use the pattern below to cut the dragon's scales. Attach the scales to your costume with tape. Start at the bottom with the smaller scales and overlap each row, ending with the larger scales on top.

Cut as many of this size scale as you can from the garbage bag.

Here's what you do to make the tail:

1 Use 2 large paper grocery bags, 3 medium-sized paper bags, and 2 paper lunch bags for the tail. Fold a crease in the bottom of each bag as shown.

2 Lay the bags out on the floor in a line with the top of each bag touching the bottom of the next one. (Large bags should go at the top; small bags at the bottom of the tail.) Staple the bags together as shown.

3 Make two small holes near the top of the first bag. Tie a string through each hole. Use this string to tie the tail around your shoulders.

4 Put on your dragon body, allowing the tail to hang out at the back. Tape the front of the body shut.

5 Put on your dragon head and a pair of gloves. You're ready to go!

FAMILY ROOTS

Some of the best ideas for plays come from real stories. Are there any good stories in your family? Why not ask the older people in your family and find out? They may give you a good idea for a play. Use the costumes on the following pages, when you perform your play.

Here's what you need:

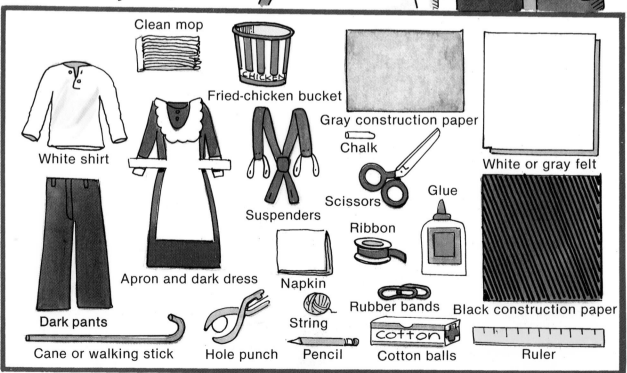

Clean mop

Fried-chicken bucket

Gray construction paper

White or gray felt

White shirt

Chalk

Scissors

Glue

Suspenders

Ribbon

Apron and dark dress

Napkin

Black construction paper

Dark pants

Rubber bands

String

Cane or walking stick

Hole punch

Pencil

Cotton balls

Ruler

36

Here's what you do to make Great-grandpa's hat:

1 Wash and dry the chicken bucket. Place the bottom of the bucket onto a sheet of black construction paper. Trace the circle with chalk. Cut out the circle and glue it to the bottom of the bucket.

2 Place the top of the bucket on a sheet of black paper. Trace the circle with chalk. Set the bucket aside.

3 Draw a larger circle around the traced circle—about 3″ wider all around. This will be the brim of your hat. Cut along the line of the larger circle.

4 Draw a smaller circle inside the traced circle—about 1-½″ smaller all around. Cut along the line of the smaller circle. Snip tab lines from the inside rim to the traced line as shown.

5 Cover the bucket with a strip of black construction paper and glue in place.

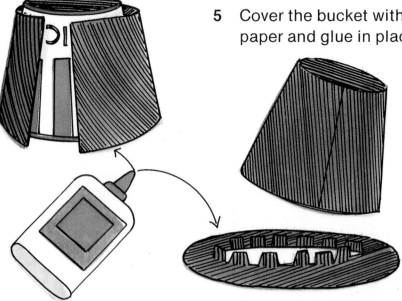

6 Fold the tabs up all around the rim. Spread glue on the outside of the tabs. Press the tabs to the inside rim of the chicken bucket.

Here's what you do to make Great-grandpa's beard:

1 Copy the beard pattern onto a folded sheet of gray construction paper.

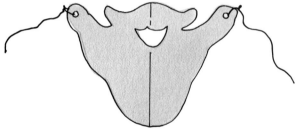

2 Punch a hole through both layers of the paper.

3 Unfold the beard. Tie a length of string to each hole.

4 To make the white hair, stretch out about 25 cotton balls. Spread glue over the paper beard and glue the cotton to the paper.

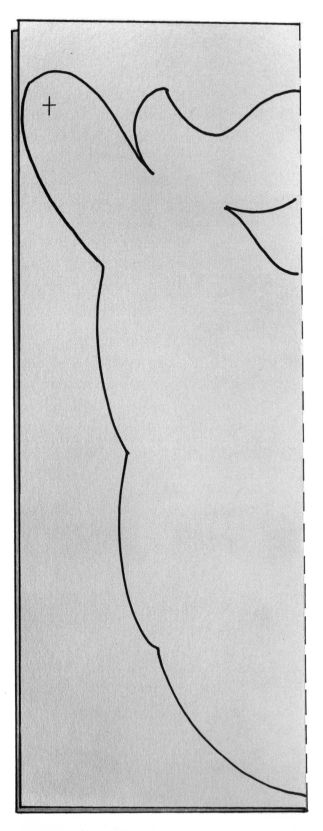

Here's what you do to make Great-grandma's wig:

1   Take a clean mop and separate it in half as shown. Place the parted mop on your head. Adjust the strands, so that they hang like hair.

2   Grasp the strands from the back of your head. Tie a rubber band around the bunch like a ponytail.

3   Cut a 6″ × 6″ square of white or gray felt. Wrap it over the ponytail. Then, wrap a second rubber band around the felt.

To make the lace collar, see the following pages.

Here's what you do to make Great-grandma's collar:

1 Cut a paper napkin in half...then fold it in half, lengthwise...then in half again, crosswise...and in half once more.

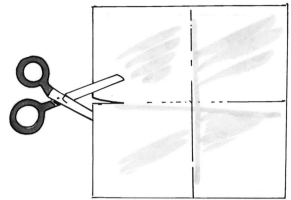

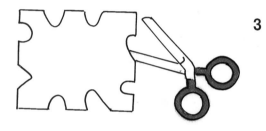

2 Cut small designs along the four edges of the folded napkin.

3 Fold the napkin diagonally to form a triangle. Cut a shape in the center of the fold as shown.

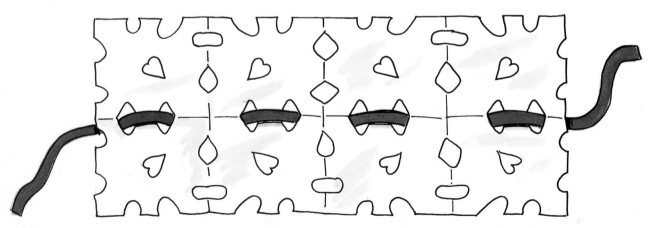

4 Open the napkin into the shape of a long rectangle. Cut a ribbon 2 feet long and thread the ribbon through the center of the design. Allow enough ribbon on either end of the rectangle to be able to tie the collar around your neck.

To make Great-grandpa's costume complete, wear a white shirt, dark pants, suspenders, and carry a walking stick!

To make Great-grandma's costume complete, wear a long dark dress and a white apron. It'll look great with your lace collar!

SPACE TRAVELER'S GEAR

Here's the perfect outfit for walking on the moon or traveling to faraway planets. This outfit has two sections: the head gear and a body suit.

Here's what you need:

Scissors

Glue

Aluminum foil

Ruler

Pencil

Colored construction paper

Crayons or markers

Paper bag

Here's what you do to make the head gear:

Draw an oval this size, about 4-½″ up from the bottom of the bag.

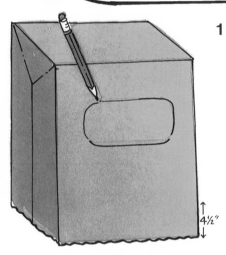

1 Pierce the bag carefully, and cut around the outline of the oval shape.

2 Slit each corner of the bag up about 4-½″ from the bottom.

4½″

3 Fold the tabs up as shown.

4 Decorate the head gear. Cut knobs and dials from aluminum foil or construction paper. Then cut small rectangles and glue them around the oval opening. Use markers or crayons to draw the gauges.

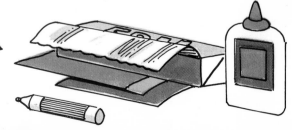

Here's what you need:

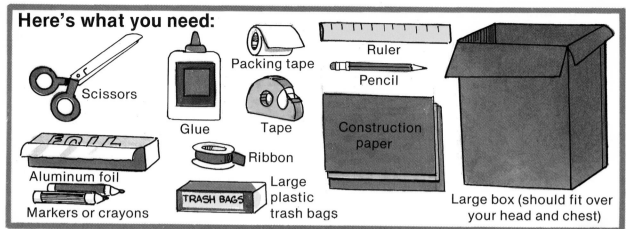

Scissors

Glue

Tape

Packing tape

Ruler

Pencil

Construction paper

Aluminum foil

Ribbon

Markers or crayons

Large plastic trash bags

Large box (should fit over your head and chest)

SPACE TRAVELER'S SUIT
Here's what you do:

1 Cut off the flaps on the open end of the box.

2 Draw rectangles on opposite sides of the box. Make the rectangles 4″ wide and 2″ down from the closed end of the box. Starting at the open end, cut out the rectangles.

3 Draw a 7″ square in the center of the closed end of the box. Cut the square by starting at the top of one of the rectangles. (Tape the cut you've made with packing tape.)

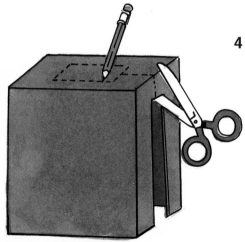

4 Decorate the box suit with knobs and dials made of construction paper and aluminum foil. Cut out your designs and glue them to the box. Use crayons or markers to add details.

5 To make the arms of the suit, lay 2 large plastic garbage bags out on a flat surface. Cut a small semi-circle in the center of the closed end of each bag.

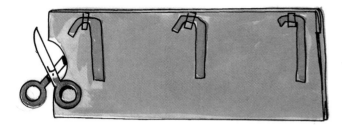

6 Cut 6 pieces of ribbon, each 18″ long.
Tape 3 ribbons to the side of each bag.
Start at the closed end of each bag, and tape the first ribbon 1″ up from the side of the bag. (Tape each ribbon across its center as shown.) Tape the second ribbon 11″ up from the first. Tape the third ribbon 11″ up from the second.

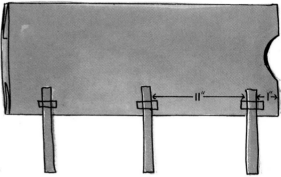

7 Now tape the bags to the box suit. Tape the open end of the trash bag against the inside of the rectangle, so the bag stretches out of the box like an arm.

You need only to tape a small portion of the bag to the rectangle—just enough to hold the bag in place.

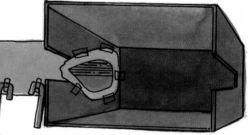

8 Put the box over your head and your arms through the bags. Tie the ribbons around your arms, making gathers in the bags. Add a pair of gloves to the outfit. With this suit, your gloves, and head gear, you're ready for outer space!

EXTRATERRESTRIAL MASK

While visiting another planet, you might meet someone who lives there. Here's a mask to wear the next time you greet an extraterrestrial friend!

Here's what you need:

Scissors

Hole punch

Empty margarine container

2 Styrofoam cups

Markers or crayons

Pipe cleaners

Here's what you do:

1 Cut off the bottoms of 2 styrofoam cups. Punch holes

in the rim of each cup as shown. Then, punch holes in the margarine container as shown.

2 Overlap 2 pipe cleaners by about 2″ and wrap the overlapping ends tightly around one another.

3 Pass the joined pipe cleaners through points A, B, C, and D of the styrofoam cups. Criss-cross the pipe cleaners between the two cups and circle the ends as shown to form the antennae.

4 Pass another pipe cleaner through point E of the first styrofoam cup, points F and G of the margarine container, and point H of the second styrofoam cup. Twist the ends of the pipe cleaner at points E and H, so it will not slip through the holes.

5 Tie one pipe cleaner to the side hole in each cup. Twist each pipe cleaner as shown.

6 Use markers to decorate your extraterrestrial mask.

EAU CLAIRE DISTRICT LIBRARY